DISCOVERING Space

THE FAR PLANETS

Ian Graham

W

FRANKLIN WATTS

An Appleseed Editions book

published in 2007 by Franklin Watts

Franklin Watts
338 Euston Road, London NW1 3BH

Franklin Watts Australia
Level 17/207 Kent St, Sydney, NSW 2000

© 2007 Appleseed Editions

Appleseed Editions Ltd
Well House, Friars Hill, Guestling, East Sussex TN35 4ET

Created by Q2A Media
Series Editor: Honor Head
Designers: Diksha Khatri, Ashita Murgai
Picture Researchers: Lalit Dalal, Jyoti Sachdev

ISBN   978 0 7496 7548 6

Dewey classification: 523.4

All words in **bold** can be found in the glossary on page 30.

A CIP catalogue for this book is available from the British Library.

Picture credits
t=top b=bottom c=centre l=left r=right m=middle
Cover images: Science Photo Library/ Photolibrary: tr, Nasa, ESA, J. Clarke (Boston University, USA), and Z. Levay (STScI): tl,
Calvin J. Hamilton/ Nasa: bl, Nasa/ JPL-Caltech: br, small images: Nasa/ JPL-Caltech: cl, mr. Calvin J. Hamilton/ Nasa: 4, 5l, 5r,
6l, 7b, Science Photo Library/ Photolibrary: 5t, 6-7 (background), 14, 15b, 18, 19t, 21b, 22, 25b, 27, Nasa: 8, 10, 16, 19b,
23, 25t, Nasa/ JPL-Caltech: 9t, 11, 15t, 17, 20b, 26, Corbis: 13, Boeing Satellite Systems: 21b,
The International Astronomical Union/ Martin Kornmesser/ Science Photo Library: 24.

Printed in China

Franklin Watts is a division of Hachette Children's Books

Contents

The far planets

Eight **planets** fly in endless **orbit** around the Sun.
The four closest to the Sun are small planets.
The four planets furthest from the Sun are much
bigger. These are known as the far planets and they
are Jupiter, Saturn, Uranus and Neptune.

Jupiter

Saturn

The gas giants

The far planets are surrounded by a mixture of gases called an
atmosphere. The **gravity** of each planet holds the atmosphere
around the planet in place. Because the far planets are so big,
they are also called **gas giants**. These planets are huge, so their
gravity holds a lot of gas around them, which means each
planet has a very thick atmosphere.

Spotlight on
space

More than 150 moons orbit the eight planets of the Solar System. Nearly all of them circle the four far planets. Jupiter has 63 moons, more than any other planet. Saturn, the beautiful, ringed planet, has nearly as many, with a total of 56.

Viewed from the far planets, the Solar System looks different. The Sun is a small, distant star.

Uranus

Neptune

The four far planets are icy and cold because they orbit so far from the Sun.

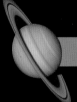

The first dwarf planet

Until 2006, there was a ninth planet called Pluto, which was beyond Neptune. Pluto was the smallest planet and the same size as lots of other objects in space. Many **astronomers** thought that if Pluto was a planet, the other objects should be named as planets as well. This would give the Solar System more than 150 extra planets. So, in 2006, it was decided to call Pluto a **dwarf planet**. Many of the other objects may also be named as dwarf planets.

Jupiter

If you look up into the sky at night and see a star shining brighter than all the others, it might not be a star at all. You might be looking at the giant planet Jupiter.

Mighty planet

Jupiter is the biggest of all the planets in the Solar System. It is two and a half times the weight of all the other planets added together. Jupiter is 11 times wider than Earth and it takes up as much space as 1,321 Earths.

Jupiter facts

Size across the middle	142,796 kilometres
Distance from the Sun	778 million kilometres
Gravity	twice the strength of the Earth's gravity
Atmosphere	mainly hydrogen and helium
Moons	at least 63
Length of day	about 10 hours
Length of year	11.8 Earth years

Jupiter is four times brighter than the brightest star, but it gives out no light of its own. It appears as a round disc in the night sky and is so bright because it reflects lots of sunlight.

Great Red Spot

Hundreds of huge storms race around Jupiter. The biggest is the Great Red Spot which is a giant **hurricane**, bigger than two whole Earths. It was first seen more than 300 years ago and is still there.

Jupiter is made mostly of hydrogen. Inside Jupiter, the hydrogen is squashed so hard that it changes to liquid. Under Jupiter's atmosphere, there is a vast ocean of liquid hydrogen.

Winds blow around Jupiter amazingly fast. They are four or five times as fast as a hurricane on Earth.

The English scientist Robert Hooke was the first person to see Jupiter's Great Red Spot, in 1664.

Jupiter's moons

In 1610, Italian astronomer Galileo Galilei looked at Jupiter and saw four moons around it. Since then, other astronomers have found many more moons close to Jupiter. Today, the total stands at over 60 moons but there may be even more.

Galileo's moons

The four moons that Galileo saw are the biggest of Jupiter's many moons. These four moons are called Ganymede, Callisto, Io and Europa. Today they are still known as the **Galilean moons**. Ganymede is the biggest moon in the whole Solar System. It is bigger than the planet Mercury.

The Galilean moons	
Moon names	**Size across the middle**
Ganymede ▶	5,262 kilometres
Callisto ▶	4,821 kilometres
Io ▶	3,643 kilometres
Europa ▶	3,122 kilometres

Ganymede and Callisto are mostly ice. Io has lots of volcanoes. Europa is rock covered by ice.

Ganymede   Callisto   Io   Europa

Jupiter is surrounded by a dark ring and cloudy bands. They are all made of dust knocked off small moons when rocks from space crash into them.

How many moons?

By the 1970s, astronomers using more powerful telescopes found another nine moons circling Jupiter. In 1979, the *Voyager 1* space probe found another three. Astronomers kept searching and found another 47. Many of these are very small, some are less than ten kilometres across. Altogether there are now 63 moons.

Spotlight on
space

The pull of gravity from Jupiter and its moons squashes and stretches Io. This heats it up. The heat bursts out through volcanoes. There are more than 500 volcanoes on Io.

Exploring Jupiter

The exploration of Jupiter began in the early 1970s. The first space probe to visit Jupiter was *Pioneer 10*. As the probe flew past Jupiter in 1973, it took the first close-up photographs of the giant planet.

Galileo in orbit

After *Pioneer 10*, three more space probes flew past Jupiter, *Pioneer 11*, *Voyager 1* and *Voyager 2*. Then a probe called *Galileo* was carefully steered into orbit around Jupiter. The probe was named after the first scientist to look at Jupiter through a telescope, Galileo Galilei.

Camera

Radio dish

The *Galileo* space probe spent several years studying Jupiter. It sent back pictures and other information to Earth.

Galileo mission

Launched	▶	18 October 1989
Flew past Venus	▶	19 February 1990
Flew past Earth	▶	8 December 1990
Flew past Earth again	▶	8 December 1992
Released mini probe	▶	13 July 1995
Arrived at Jupiter	▶	7 December 1995
Mission ended	▶	21 September 2003

The coloured bands of Jupiter's clouds are caused by its fast spinning.

Spotlight on space

Galileo used the pull of gravity of each planet it passed to pick up enough speed for its journey to Jupiter. When it arrived, it spent nearly eight years orbiting Jupiter.

Jupiter probe

As *Galileo* flew towards Jupiter, it released a barrel-sized probe. The probe plunged through Jupiter's atmosphere. It found that Jupiter was made of the same gases as the Sun, mainly hydrogen and **helium**. The probe also discovered huge thunderstorms raging in the planet's atmosphere, far bigger than any storm on Earth.

Saturn

Saturn is the Solar System's second biggest planet after Jupiter and also the second biggest gas giant. It is the sixth planet from the Sun and has the most amazing rings.

Distant giant

Saturn is not as big as Jupiter, but it is still a giant. It is more than nine times wider than Earth. Like Jupiter, Saturn is made of the same material as stars but it did not grow big enough to become a star.

Spotlight on
space

Until the 1970s astronomers thought Saturn had only nine moons. Since then, four space probes have visited Saturn and more powerful telescopes have been used to study it. Lots more moons have been found. By 2006, the total was 56.

Saturn is the lightest planet — it is lighter than water. It is the only planet that would float.

Saturn facts

Size across the middle	▶	120,000 kilometres
Distance from the Sun	▶	1,433 million kilometres
Gravity	▶	almost the same strength as Earth's
Atmosphere	▶	mainly hydrogen and helium
Moons	▶	at least 56
Length of day	▶	nearly 11 hours
Length of year	▶	about 29 Earth years

Ice worlds

Saturn's moons are all made of rock and ice but they are all different. Iapetus is bright on one side and dark on the other side. Mimas has a huge **crater** made by a boulder which crashed into it and nearly broke it apart. Enceladus has water bubbling up on to the surface from inside. The biggest of Saturn's moons, Titan, has a thick atmosphere. Hyperion has a flattened shape – from the way it spins, scientists think a **meteorite** may have crashed into it recently.

Scientists are studying Saturn's moons to see what they can find out about Saturn's history.

Saturn's rings

All the giant gas planets are surrounded by rings, but Saturn's rings are by far the biggest and brightest. They are the only rings that can be seen clearly from Earth.

Ice and rock

Saturn's rings look like a solid disc but they are actually made of countless billions of pieces of rock and ice. These range in size from specks of dust to chunks of ice the size of a house or even bigger.

Saturn casts a shadow across its rings.

Ring facts

Size of all the rings together	▶	280,000 kilometres wide
Thickness	▶	up to 1 kilometre
Discovered in	▶	1610
Discovered by	▶	Galileo Galilei

Disappearing rings

Saturn tilts like a spinning top leaning over. When it tilts towards Earth, the rings look big, broad and bright. At other times, the rings look smaller and thinner. The way they look depends on how much Saturn is tilted.

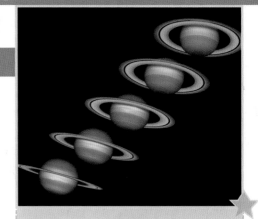

The rings around Saturn seem to change size and shape when we see them from different angles.

Spotlight on
space

Saturn's rings may be the remains of a moon, asteroid or comet that was smashed to bits when it hit something. Or they could be pieces of ice and rock that did not form into a moon.

Saturn's gravity keeps dust, rocks and ice swirling in rings around it.

Mission to Saturn

By 1981, three space probes had flown past Saturn. They gave us the first close-up pictures of the planet as they hurtled past. Then, in 2004, a new probe called *Cassini* was steered into orbit around Saturn to spend years studying it in detail.

Heavyweight explorer

Cassini is the biggest **spacecraft** ever sent to explore a planet. It is nearly seven metres long and weighs 5.6 tonnes on the launch pad. Most of this weight is fuel. The big radio dish at one end receives instructions from Earth and sends pictures and other information back to Earth.

The huge *Cassini* probe is tested by scientists.

As *Cassini* nears Saturn, its rocket fires to slow it down, so Saturn's gravity can pull it into orbit.

Cassini mission

Launched	▶	15 October 1997
Flew past Venus	▶	27 April 1998
Flew past Venus again	▶	24 June 1999
Flew past Earth	▶	18 August 1999
Flew past Jupiter	▶	30 December 2000
Entered Saturn orbit	▶	1 July 2004
Huygens probe landed on Titan	▶	14 January 2005

Surprising discoveries

Cassini has made lots of exciting discoveries. It has found new moons and rings. It spotted huge clumps of ice several kilometres across in the rings. The biggest surprise was on the moon, Enceladus. The probe discovered **geysers** gushing ice into space.

Spotlight on space

As Cassini flew towards Saturn, it released a mini probe called Huygens, which plunged into the atmosphere of Saturn's moon, Titan. It took the first photographs of Titan's surface.

Uranus

Uranus is the seventh planet from the Sun and the third biggest planet in the Solar System. Uranus is so far away from Earth that it looks like a star. Only one space probe, *Voyager 2*, has ever visited it.

Blue haze

Like Jupiter and Saturn, Uranus is made mainly of hydrogen and helium. But Uranus looks different. The main difference is its colour. **Methane gas** in its atmosphere gives it a hazy blue-green colour.

Uranus is surrounded by about a dozen rings.

Uranus facts

Size across the middle	▶	51,800 kilometres
Distance from the Sun	▶	2,872 million kilometres
Gravity	▶	less than the strength of Earth's
Atmosphere	▶	mainly hydrogen and helium
Moons	▶	at least 27
Length of day	▶	just over 17 hours
Length of year	▶	nearly 84 Earth years

Lying down

Uranus lies on its side. One **pole** faces the Sun for 42 years, then the other pole faces the Sun for 42 years. No one knows why this is so. If something big enough to knock Uranus over had hit it, the whole planet would have burst apart. So Uranus was probably hit by lots of smaller objects, each giving it a small extra tilt.

The biggest of Uranus's moons is called Titania. It is about 1,600 kilometres across — less than half the size of our Moon.

Spotlight on
space

Uranus is the first planet to be discovered by using a telescope. The astronomer William Herschel stumbled across it by accident in 1781 when he was studying some stars.

Uranus has no cloud bands, unlike Jupiter, because it is cooler.

Dish antenna

The *Voyager 2* space probe flew past Uranus in 1986.

Neptune

Neptune is the smallest and most distant of the four gas giants. It was not discovered until 1846. Nearly 150 years later, a space probe crossed the Solar System from Earth to take a closer look at this fascinating planet.

Blue world

Neptune looks like Uranus because the two planets have a few things in common. They are roughly the same size; the length of a day on each planet is almost the same and, like Uranus, Neptune is blue because of methane gas in its atmosphere.

The temperature of Neptune's blue atmosphere is about −200 degrees Celsius.

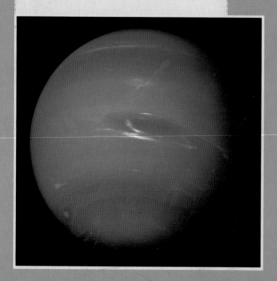

Neptune facts

Size across the middle	▶	48,500 kilometres
Distance from the Sun	▶	4,495 million kilometres
Gravity	▶	a little stronger than Earth's
Atmosphere	▶	mainly hydrogen and helium
Moons	▶	at least 13
Length of day	▶	16 hours
Length of year	▶	about 164 Earth years

Spotlight on
space

When astronomers studied Uranus, it did not move exactly as it should. It was as if it was being tugged by an even more distant planet. Astronomers examined the space around Uranus and found Neptune.

The cameras on *Voyager 2* recorded wispy white clouds forming over Neptune and disappearing within a few minutes.

Disappearing spot

A space probe called *Voyager 2* flew past Neptune in 1989. Its cameras saw a huge dark mark as big as Earth on Neptune's surface. It became known as the Great Dark Spot. But in 1996, when scientists tried to examine it through the Hubble Space Telescope, the Great Dark Spot had disappeared.

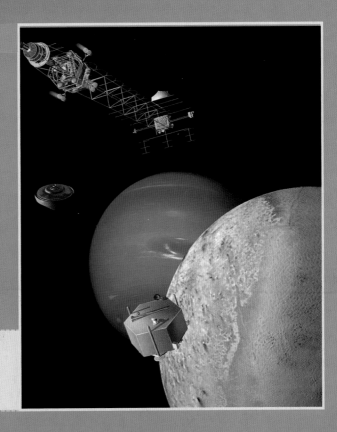

Neptune's biggest moon, Triton (seen here in the foreground), is the coldest object found in the Solar System so far.

Grand tour

Once every 175 years, the four giant gas planets line up in space. When they do this they are in the perfect position for a space probe to fly past two, three or all four of them.

Space voyagers

In 1977, two space probes, *Voyager 1* and *Voyager 2*, were sent on a grand tour of the far planets. Space probe *Voyager 2* took a different path through space. *Voyager 1* flew past Jupiter and Saturn. *Voyager 2* flew past all four of the giant gas planets.

The pull of gravity of each planet put each *Voyager* on course for the next planet.

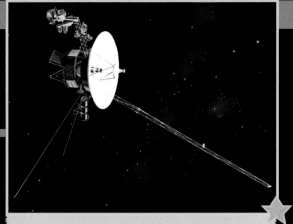

The *Voyager* space probes are expected to carry on working until about 2020.

If aliens ever find one of the Voyager probes drifting through space they will find a disc of recorded sounds from Earth and a map showing where Earth is.

Far, far away

Voyagers 1 and *2* are heading out of the Solar System towards the stars. *Voyager 1* is now the furthest spacecraft from Earth. By the middle of 2006, it was 15 billion kilometres from Earth. Both spacecraft are flying away at more than 20,000 kilometres per second.

Voyager missions

		Voyager 1	Voyager 2
Launched	▶	5 September 1977	20 August 1977
Flew past Jupiter	▶	5 March 1979	9 July 1979
Flew past Saturn	▶	12 November 1980	25 August 1981
Flew past Uranus	▶		24 January 1986
Flew past Neptune	▶		24 August 1989

Dwarf planets

In 2006, astronomers decided on a new name for the smaller, round, planet-like objects in the Solar System. They are now called dwarf planets. This group includes Pluto, which had been the Solar System's ninth planet.

Ceres and Eris

As well as Pluto, two other dwarf planets have been named. They are Ceres and Eris. Ceres is the biggest object ever found in the **asteroid belt**, a region of space between Mars and Jupiter where boulders orbit the Sun. Eris is about three times further from the Sun than Pluto and is bigger than Pluto. Eris is the biggest object found in the whole Solar System since the planet Neptune in 1846.

Eris

Ceres

Ceres contains about a third of all the matter in the asteroid belt.

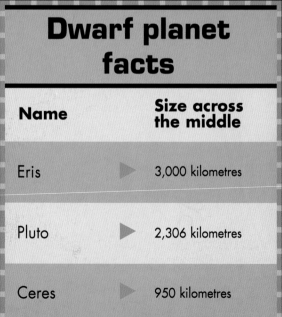

Dwarf planet facts

Name	Size across the middle
Eris	3,000 kilometres
Pluto	2,306 kilometres
Ceres	950 kilometres

The *New Horizons* space probe will approach Pluto and its moons in 2015.

On 19 January 2006, the *New Horizons* space probe left Earth on its long journey to Pluto. It is the first space probe to visit this distant dwarf planet. The flight will take nine and a half years. It will fly past Pluto taking photographs and studying Pluto's thin atmosphere.

Spotlight on
space

To be called a dwarf planet an object must be big enough for its gravity to pull it into a ball shape. Objects bigger than about 200 kilometres across the middle have strong enough gravity to do this.

Pluto | Charon

The biggest of Pluto's three moons, Charon, is so big that it could also become a dwarf planet when more is known about it.

The future

Rockets are used to power space probes to the far planets. But rockets need a lot of fuel to make them work. Future probes to the far planets may be powered in many different ways. Some of them may even travel like sailing ships.

Space power

The *Deep Space 1* space probe was powered by a new type of engine – not a rocket but an **ion engine**. The ion engine was able to push the space probe to ten times the speed of a rocket and keep it working for a longer time.

Glowing gas rushing from an ion engine pushes the space probe as gently as a single sheet of paper pressing on someone's hand.

Deep Space 1 mission

Launched	▶	24 October 1998
Flew past comet Braille	▶	29 July 1999
Flew past comet Borrelly	▶	22 September 2001
Mission ended	▶	18 December 2001

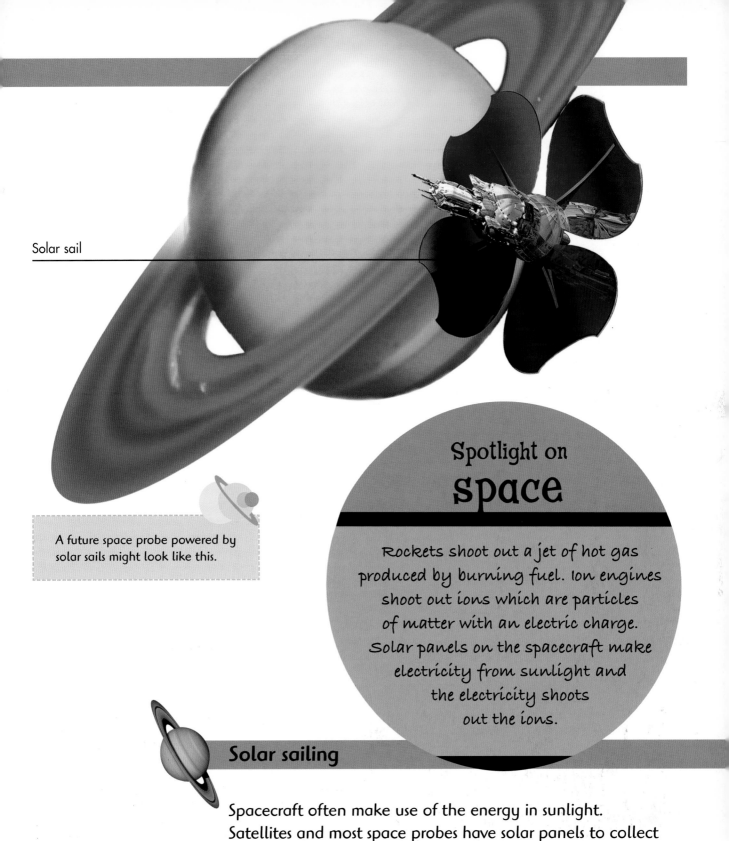

Solar sail

A future space probe powered by solar sails might look like this.

Rockets shoot out a jet of hot gas produced by burning fuel. Ion engines shoot out ions which are particles of matter with an electric charge. Solar panels on the spacecraft make electricity from sunlight and the electricity shoots out the ions.

Solar sailing

Spacecraft often make use of the energy in sunlight. Satellites and most space probes have solar panels to collect sunlight and change it into electricity. But sunlight can also move a spacecraft. When sunlight hits something, it gives it a tiny push. A spacecraft with a giant mirror a kilometre across would get a big enough push to move it through space. Huge mirrors used like this are called solar sails.

Timeline

1610
The Italian astronomer and scientist Galileo Galilei looks at Jupiter through a telescope and discovers four moons orbiting it.

1655
The Dutch mathematician Christiaan Huygens discovers Saturn's biggest moon, Titan.

1671
The Italian astronomer Giovanni Cassini discovers Saturn's moon, Iapetus.

1672
Giovanni Cassini discovers Saturn's moon, Rhea.

1675
Giovanni Cassini discovers the main gap between Saturn's rings.

1781
German astronomer William Herschel discovers the planet Uranus.

1789
William Herschel discovers Saturn's moons, Mimas and Enceladus.

1846
Neptune is discovered by the German scientists Johann Galle and Heinrich D'Arrest, using calculations made by the French astronomer, Urbain Le Verrier.

1848
British astronomer William Lassell discovers Neptune's moon, Triton.

1850
One of Saturn's rings, called the Crepe ring, is discovered.

1857
Scientists work out that Saturn's rings must be made from lots of separate particles.

1930
Pluto is discovered by American astronomer, Clyde Tombaugh.

1944
Saturn's biggest moon, Titan, is found to have an atmosphere.

1972
Pioneer 10 is launched to the far planets.

1973
Pioneer 11 is launched.

Pioneer 10 is the first spacecraft to fly past Jupiter.

1974
Pioneer 11 flies past Jupiter.

1977
Rings around Uranus are discovered.

1978
Pluto's biggest moon, Charon, is discovered.

1979
Voyagers 1 and *2* fly past Jupiter.

Pioneer 11 flies past Saturn.

1980
Voyager 1 flies past Saturn.

1981
Voyager 2 flies past Saturn.

1986
Voyager 2 flies past Uranus.

1989
Voyager 2 flies past Neptune.

The *Galileo* space probe is launched.

1995

Galileo drops a mini probe into Jupiter's atmosphere just before it goes into orbit around Jupiter.

1996

The Hubble Space telescope photographs the surface of Saturn's moon, Titan.

1997

The *Cassini* space probe is launched on a mission to Saturn.

2002

Galileo begins a tour of Jupiter's moons by flying past the planet's biggest moon, Ganymede.

2003

Galileo's mission is ended by sending it plunging into Pluto's atmosphere.

2004

Cassini flies past Saturn's moons, Phoebe and Dion.

2005

Cassini flies past Saturn's moons, Iapetus and Enceladus.

Two new moons belonging to Pluto are found.

Cassini's Huygens mini probe lands on Titan and sends back photographs of its surface.

2006

The *New Horizons* space probe to Pluto is launched.

Glossary

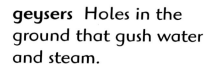

antenna The part of a radio or radio telescope that sends or receives radio waves.

asteroid A large piece of rock, smaller than a planet, in orbit around the Sun.

asteroid belt A region of asteroids between Mars and Jupiter.

astronomers Scientists who study astronomy.

atmosphere The gas around a planet or moon. The Earth's atmosphere is made of air.

comet A small lump made of ice and rock travelling through space which has a long bright tail when it comes close to the Sun.

crater A shallow circular dip in the surface of a planet or moon caused by a space rock smashing into it.

dwarf planet A large round object orbiting a star, but not big enough to be called a planet.

Galilean moons The four biggest moons of Jupiter, seen by Galileo in 1610 – Ganymede, Callisto, Io and Europa.

gas giants Huge planets made mainly of gas. Jupiter, Saturn, Uranus and Neptune are gas giants.

geysers Holes in the ground that gush water and steam.

gravity An invisible force that pulls things towards each other. Earth's gravity pulls us down on to the ground. The Sun's gravity holds the planets in their orbits.

helium The second lightest chemical element and the second most plentiful element after hydrogen. Helium is found in stars.

hurricane A huge revolving storm with wind blowing at 120 kph or more.

hydrogen The simplest, lightest and most plentiful of all the chemical elements. Stars are mostly made of hydrogen.

ion engine A type of engine that uses energy from the Sun instead of a rocket to power a spacecraft.

meteorite A rock that falls on to a planet from space.

methane gas A gas found in the atmospheres of some planets. It is the gas that gives Uranus and Neptune their blue-green colouring.

moons Small objects orbiting a planet. The Earth has one moon, called the Moon.

orbit The path a planet follows through space around the Sun, or the path of a moon around a planet. Orbit can also describe the path of a spacecraft as it flies around the Sun, a planet or a moon, or the path of a satellite around a planet or a moon.

planets Big objects in orbit around a star. Planets do not give out light of their own. They shine only because they reflect light.

pole One of two points at the furthest north and south of a planet.

ring A circle or broad band of dust or ice around a planet.

Solar System The Sun, planets, moons and everything else that orbits the Sun.

spacecraft A machine sent into space. Manned spacecraft have people inside. Unmanned spacecraft have no one inside.

solar panels Parts of a spacecraft which make electricity from sunlight.

space probe An unmanned spacecraft sent away from Earth to explore part of the Solar System.

Index

WEBFINDER

http://www.bbc.co.uk/science/space/solarsystem/jupiter/index.shtml

http://www.bbc.co.uk/science/space/solarsystem/saturn/index.shtml

http://www.bbc.co.uk/science/space/solarsystem/uranus/index.shtml

http://www.bbc.co.uk/science/space/solarsystem/neptune/index.shtml

http://www.bbc.co.uk/science/space/solarsystem/pluto/index.shtml

http://www.kidsastronomy.com/solar_system.htm

http://spaceplace.nasa.gov/en/kids/sse_flipflop2.shtml

http://www.dustbunny.com/afk/planets